INTRODUC

Are you the **Ultimate Football Fan**?

This book contains 320 football quiz questions on the English Premier League, FIFA World Cup, UEFA Champions League...and many more.

Test yourself or play with your friends to see how many questions you can get right!

Bonus: This book also contains 5 fun facts on football!

CONTENT

1. GENERAL

1. What is the full form of FIFA?

2. When was football introduced in the Olympics?

3. What is an overhead kick also known as?

4. What does a clean sheet mean in football?

5. What is the name of the award for top goal scorer?

6. What is the name of the competition played annually between the winners of the FA Cup and the winners of the Premier League?

7. When was the first official international football match played?

8. Which city was FIFA founded?

9. What size is a standard football pitch?

10. What does Ballon d'Or honour?

11. What is "the Pichichi" in Spanish football?

12. What does VAR stand for in football?

13. Where is the headquarters of FIFA?

14. What is the full form of UEFA?

15. What is football called in the USA?

16. What does Ballon d'Or mean?

ANSWERS - GENERAL

1. Fédération Internationale De Football Association

2. 1900

3. Bicycle kick

4. A game where the opposing team is prevented from scoring.

5. Golden Boot

6. The Community Shield

7. 1872

8. Paris

9. 125m x 85m

10. The male player deemed to have performed the best over the previous year.

11. Award given to the top goal scorer

12. Video assistant referee

13. Zurich, Switzerland

14. Union of European Football Associations

15. Soccer

16. Golden Ball

FUN FACT - CUJU

Cuju is an ancient Chinese ball game that dates back to the Han Dynasty (206 BCE - 220 CE). It involved two teams competing to kick a leather ball into a net or between two poles without using their hands. Cuju was a popular pastime in China for centuries and was often played for entertainment or as part of military training exercises.

The game of Cuju bears many similarities to modern football. Both games involve teams trying to score by kicking a ball into a designated area, and both require skill, strategy, and teamwork. However, there are some key differences between the two sports, such as the size and shape of the ball, the number of players on a team, and the rules governing the use of hands and other body parts.

While Cuju is no longer widely played today, it is considered an important predecessor to modern football and has helped to shape the development of the sport over time. Many historians and sports enthusiasts view Cuju as an early example of the global phenomenon of football and recognize its role in the evolution of the game as we know it today.

2. ENGLISH PREMIER LEAGUE

17. Which team won the first Premier League Title?

Man u

18. In what year was the Premier League founded?

1992

19. Who was the first player to win the Premier League Player of the Season award three times?

20. Who is the youngest player to score a hat-trick in the Premier League?

21. Which team was Wayne Rooney playing against when he scored his first Premier League goal?

22. Who is the Premier League's all-time leading scorer?

allan Shearer

23. Who scored the fastest Premier League goal at 7.69 seconds?

?

24. How many clubs competed in the first Premier League?

24

25. Who was the first manager to win the Premier League in his first season in charge? *busby*

26. What is the nickname of Liverpool Football Club? *reds*

27. When did Sir Alex Ferguson become Manchester United manager?

28. What is the maximum number of substitutions a team can make in a single Premier League match? *3 or 5*

29. What is the name of the stadium that was the home of Arsenal Football Club between 1913 and 2006? *nirbury*

30. Which 3 players shared the Premier League Golden Boot in 2018-2019?

31. Who has made the most Premier League appearances?

32. Which football stadium is known as the Theatre of Dreams?

33. Who is the highest-scoring foreign player in Premier League history?

34. Who was the manager of Arsenal when they won the Premier League in 2003-04 without losing a single game?

35. What is the minimum number of players a team must have on the field at all times, including the goalkeeper?

36. Who scored the first ever Premier League goal?

37. Who was the first African player to win the Premier League Player of the Season award?

38. Which 3 players share the record for most number of Premier League red cards (8)?

39. Who was the first player to win the Premier League Young Player of the Season award three times?

40. What colours did Manchester United wear before adopting red?

41. Who was the first player to win the Premier League Golden Boot award three times in a row?

42. Who was the manager of Liverpool when they won the Premier League for the first time?

43. Who scored the most own goals in the Premier League?

44. Who won the 2019-2020 English Premier League title?

45. Who was the first sponsor for the Premier League?

46. Who was the first non-English player to score 100 goals in the Premier League?

47. Which city is Aston Villa based in?

48. How many times did Sir Alex Ferguson win the Premier League?

49. How many teams are promoted to the Premier League from the Championship each season?

50. Which year was Manchester City founded?

51. Who was the first manager to win the Premier League with two different clubs?

52. Who was the first player to score 5 goals in a Premier League match?

53. Which manager is famous for giving his players "the Hairdryer Treatment"?

54. Who was the first player to reach 300 Premier League appearances for a single club?

55. Who was the first foreign manager to win the Premier League?

56. Who was the first player to reach 50 Premier League goals in fewer than 100 appearances?

57. Which is the first team to hit 100 points in a season?

58. Who was the first player to reach 400 Premier League appearances for a single club?

59. Which team has the longest unbeaten run in the Premier League?

60. How many teams are relegated from the Premier League to the Championship each season?

61. Which year was Liverpool founded?

62. What was the first team to be relegated from the Premier League in its inaugural season?

63. Who has won the most Premier League titles?

64. Who are the "Top Four" teams in 2000s?

ANSWERS – ENGLISH PREMIER LEAGUE

17. Manchester United

18. 1992

19. Cristiano Ronaldo (2007-08, 2008-09, 2010-11)

20. James Vaughan (16 years & 271 days)

21. Arsenal

22. Alan Shearer

23. Shane Long

24. 22

25. José Mourinho (Chelsea, 2004-05)

26. The Reds

27. 1986

28. 3

29. Highbury Stadium

30. Pierre-Emerick Aubameyang, Mohamed Salah and Sadio Mane

31. Gareth Barry

32. Old Trafford

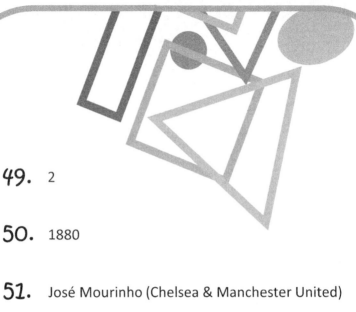

49. 2

50. 1880

51. José Mourinho (Chelsea & Manchester United)

52. Andy Cole (for Manchester United against Ipswich Town in 1995)

53. Sir Alex Ferguson

54. Ryan Giggs (Manchester United)

55. Arsène Wenger (Arsenal)

56. Andrew Cole (65 appearances)

57. Manchester City (with 100 points in the 2017-18 season)

58. Gary Speed (Everton)

59. Arsenal (with 49 games unbeaten from May 2003 to October 2004)

60. 3

61. 1892

62. Nottingham Forest

63. Manchester United

64. Arsenal, Chelsea, Liverpool and Manchester United

FUN FACT – CONFRONTING THE BULLY

In 2011, Manchester City striker Mario Balotelli made headlines when he agreed to accompany a young fan to his school to confront a bully who had been targeting him.

Balotelli arrived at the school with Marshall and his mother, and together they confronted the bullies. The situation was defused, and the bullies apologized for their behavior. Balotelli also spent time with Marshall, giving him advice and encouraging him to stand up for himself in the future.

The incident received widespread media attention and was seen as an example of Balotelli's kindness and willingness to use his influence to help others. It also highlighted the issue of bullying in schools and sparked discussions about how to prevent it. Balotelli's actions were widely praised by fans and the media, and he has continued to be remembered for his gesture of support towards the young fan.

3. FIFA WORLD CUP

65. Which country hosted the first ever FIFA World Cup tournament?

66. When was the first FIFA World Cup?

67. Who was the first player to win the World Cup Golden Glove award for the tournament's best goalkeeper three times?

68. Who was the manager of the England national football team that won the 1966 World Cup?

69. What is the record for the most goals scored by a team in a single World Cup tournament?

70. Who was the first player to win the World Cup Young Player award?

71. Which team is the first from Asia to quality for a FIFA World Cup?

72. How many teams competed in the first FIFA World Cup?

73. Which is the first year that England won the FIFA World Cup?

74. How many goals did England score in the 1966 FIFA World Cup Final?

75. Which is the first country to win FIFA World Cup 5 times?

76. What was the first FIFA World Cup trophy called?

77. What year was the first World Cup to feature 32 teams?

78. Which team is the only unbeaten team in the 2010 FIFA World Cup?

79. Who was the first ever player to win the Golden Foot award for the best player at the World Cup?

80. Which World Cup saw the introduction of the Golden Goal rule for the first time?

81. The 2026 FIFA World Cup is hosted in 3 different countries, which are the 3?

82. Who was the first ever player to win the World Cup Golden Boot award multiple times?

83. Who was the first African country to host the World Cup?

84. Which FIFA World Cup did David Beckham receive a red card against Argentina?

85. In what year did the World Cup expand to 24 teams?

86. Which countries hosted the 2002 FIFA World Cup?

87. Which country to ever compete in the world cup has the smallest population?

88. Who was the manager of the Netherlands team that reached the final of the 2010 FIFA World Cup?

89. Which country is the first to win 2 FIFA World Cups?

90. Who was the youngest player to score a goal in a World Cup match?

91. In which FIFA World Cup did Diego Maradona score his infamous "Hand of God" goal?

92. Who was the first player to score a hat-trick in the World Cup final?

93. Who was the first player to win the World Cup Golden Ball award for the tournament's best player twice?

94. Who was the top scorer of the 2018 World Cup?

95. Who won the 2014 FIFA World Cup?

96. Who was the first player to win the World Cup Silver Ball award for the tournament's second-best player twice?

97. What was the score in the first ever World Cup final in 1930?

98. Which team first feature substitutes in FIFA World Cup Finals?

99. Who was the first player to score in four World Cup tournaments?

100. What country hosted the 2022 World Cup?

101. Which year did Thierry Henry first participate in the FIFA World Cup?

102. What was the name of the first African team to reach the World Cup quarter-finals?

103. Which country hosted the 2018 FIFA World Cup?

104. Who was the leading scorer in the 2002 FIFA World Cup?

105. Which country hosted the 1966 FIFA World Cup, where England won the World Cup title?

106. Who was the first Asian country to reach the World Cup quarter-finals?

107. Who scored the first goal in the 1930 FIFA World Cup?

108. What was the score in the first-ever World Cup match?

109. What was the highest scoring World Cup match in history?

110. What is the name of the stadium where the first ever World Cup final was played?

111. What is the name of the mascot for the 2018 FIFA World Cup in Russia?

112. Which FIFA World Cup was the most venues used?

ANSWERS – FIFA WORLD CUP

65. Uruguay

66. 1930

67. Gianluigi Buffon (2006, 2010, 2014)

68. Alf Ramsey

69. Hungary in 1954 with 27 goals

70. Pele (1958)

71. The Dutch East Indies

72. 13 teams

73. 1966

74. 4

75. Brazil

76. Jules Rimet Trophy

77. 1998

78. New Zealand

79. Mario Kempes (1978)

80. The 1998 World Cup

81. United States, Canada and Mexico

82. Miroslav Klose (2002 & 2006)

83. South Africa (2010)

84. 1998

85. 1982

86. South Korea and Japan

87. Iceland

88. Bert van Marwijk

89. Italy

90. Pelé (17 years old, 1958)

91. Mexico in 1986

92. Geoff Hurst (for England in 1966)

93. Pelé (1958 & 1962)

94. Harry Kane (England)

95. Germany

96. Zinedine Zidane (1998 & 2006)

97. Uruguay 4 - 2 Argentina

98. Mexico

99. Pelé (for Brazil in 1958, 1962, 1966, and 1970)

100. Qatar

101. 1998

102. Senegal (2002)

103. Russia

104. Ronaldo (Brazil)

105. England

106. South Korea (2002)

107. Lucien Laurent (France)

108. USA vs Belgium, 3-0

109. Austria vs. Switzerland (7-5 in 1954)

110. Estadio Centenario

111. Zabivaka

112. 20 in the FIFA World Cup 2002

FUN FACT - THE DOG

In 1962, during a football match between Brazil and England in Rio de Janeiro, a stray dog entered the field and interrupted the game. The dog ran around the pitch for a few minutes, causing a delay in the match, and then made its way towards the English player Jimmy Greaves. Greaves picked up the dog, which proceeded to urinate on him.

The incident caused a stir and led to some amusing commentary from the British media. Despite the interruption, the match continued, with Brazil winning 3-1.

The incident is now regarded as a memorable moment in football history and has been referenced in popular culture over the years. It also highlights the unpredictable nature of live events and the potential for unexpected moments to capture the attention of viewers and become part of the game's folklore.

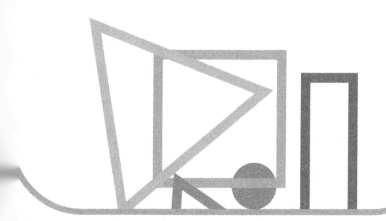

4. UEFA CHAMPIONS LEAGUE

113. What is the name of the first team to win the Champions League by a penalty shootout?

114. Who was the first player to score in three different Champions League finals?

115. What is the name of the current Champions League trophy?

116. Who was the manager of Manchester United when they won the Treble (Premier League, FA Cup, UEFA Champions League) in 1999?

Alex Ferguson

117. Who was the first team to win the Champions League in back-to-back seasons?

118. Which is the first UK club to win the European Cup?

119. Who won the Champions League in the 2019-2020 season?

120. What is the name of the award given to the player who makes the most interceptions in a single Champions League season?

121. What was the score in the first ever Champions League final?

122. What is the maximum number of teams a country can have in the Champions League?

123. Who was the first British manager to win the Champions League?

124. What is the name of the award given to the top scorer of the Champions League each season?

125. When was European Cup rebranded as Champions League?

126. Who is the Champions League all-time top scorer as of 2022?

127. Who won the first ever Champions League (after the rename) final?

128. What is the official name of the Champions League anthem?

129. Who was the first British club to win the Champions League with a all-English starting lineup?

130. Who was the manager of Barcelona when they won the UEFA Champions League in 2011?

131. Who was the first team to reach three consecutive Champions League finals?

132. What is the name of the competition held between the teams that have been eliminated from the Champions League and the Europa League?

133. Who was the first player to make 100 Champions League appearances?

134. Which Romanian team has won the Champions League?

135. Who was the first British club to reach the semi-finals of the Champions League?

136. What is the name of the stadium that hosted the 2021 Champions League final?

137. How many teams qualify for the knockout stage of the Champions League?

138. What is the name of the competition held between the winner of the Champions League and the winner of the Europa League?

139. Who was the first team to win the Champions League with a team made up entirely of players from one country?

140. Who was the manager of Chelsea when they won the UEFA Champions League in 2012?

141. Who was the first player to score in every group stage match of the Champions League?

142. Who was the first team to win the Champions League with an all-foreign starting lineup?

143. Who has provided the most assists in the Champions League as of 2022?

144. Who was the first team to win the Champions League after losing the final the previous year?

145. Who was the first team to win the European Cup five times in a row?

146. Who was the first French team to win the UEFA Champions League?

147. Which country has the most Champions League wins?

148. How many teams qualify from each group in the Champions League?

149. What was the score in the first-ever Champions League final in 1955?

150. Who was the first goalkeeper to win the Champions League Player of the Year award?

151. Who scored the fastest goal in Champions League history?

152. Which team won the 2019/2020 Champions League final behind closed doors due to COVID-19 restrictions?

ANSWERS – UEFA CHAMPIONS LEAGUE

113. Juventus

114. Cristiano Ronaldo

115. The UEFA Champions League Trophy

116. Sir Alex Ferguson

117. Real Madrid (1955-56 and 1956-57)

118. Celtic in 1966/67

119. Bayern Munich

120. The UEFA Club Defender of the Year

145. Real Madrid

146. Marseille (1993)

147. Spain

148. The top two teams from each group qualify for the knockout stages.

149. Real Madrid 4-3 Stade de Reims

150. Gianluigi Buffon

151. Roy Makaay

152. Bayern Munich

5. UEFA EUROPEAN FOOTBALL CHAMPIONSHIP

153. Which country hosted the first-ever European Championship in 1960?

154. In which year was the first penalty shoot-out in a European Championship final?

155. Which countries held the first European Championship tournament that was held in multiple countries?

156. Which year was the first European Championship held?

157. How many teams participate in the UEFA European Championship tournament?

158. What was the original name of the European Championship tournament, prior to it being changed to the UEFA European Championship in 1968?

159. Who scored the winning goal in the 2008 European Championship final?

160. What is the European Championship trophy also known as?

161. In which year did the European Championship tournament format change from 8 to 16 teams?

162. Who was the top scorer of the 2000 European Championship?

163. How many teams participated in the first UEFA European Championship tournament in 1960?

164. How often is the European Championship held?

165. Which country won the first European Championships held in 1960?

166. Who was the first player to win the European Championship, World Cup, and Champions League?

167. Who is Henri Delaunay?

168. When is the first time 24 teams played in the European Championship?

169. How many teams participated in the first European Championship tournament?

170. Who was the player of the tournament in the 2016 European Championships?

171. In which year was the first European Championship tournament to be held in multiple countries?

172. In which year did the European Championship change its name from the European Nations Cup to the UEFA European Championship?

173. What was the score of the first ever UEFA European Championship final?

174. Which teams hold the record for the most European Championships wins as of 2022?

175. Which country won the most European Championship titles before year 2000?

176. Who was the first player to score in 4 different European Championships?

177. What countries hosted the 2012 European Championships?

178. Who won the European Championship tournament in 2016?

179. Who was the manager of the Greece team that won the 2004 European Championship?

180. Who scored the winning goal in the 2012 European Championships final?

181. How many times has England won the European Championships before 2000?

182. Which country hosted the 2020 European Championship tournament?

183. How many players are allowed in a team's squad for the European Championship tournament?

184. Who scored the winning goal in the final of the 2004 European Championship?

ANSWERS – UEFA EUROPEAN FOOTBALL CHAMPIONSHIP

153. France

154. 1976

155. Belgium and Netherlands

156. 1960

157. 24

158. The European Nations' Cup

159. Fernando Torres

160. Henri Delaunay Trophy

161. 1996

162. Patrick Kluivert (Netherlands)

163. 4

164. Every 4 years

165. Soviet Union

166. Cristiano Ronaldo

167. The first General Secretary of UEFA

168. 2016

169. 4

170. Antoine Griezmann (France)

171. 2000

172. 1968

173. Soviet Union 2-1 Yugoslavia

174. Germany and Spain

175. Germany

176. Michel Platini (France)

177. Poland and Ukraine

178. Portugal

179. Otto Rehhagel

180. Fernando Torres (Spain)

181. None

182. Postponed to 2021 and hosted by 11 cities across Europe due to COVID-19 pandemic

183. 26

184. Greece's Angelos Basinas

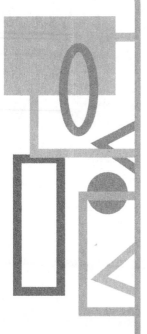

FUN FACT – THE UNDERDOG

In 1992, the UEFA European Football Championship, commonly known as Euro, was held in Sweden. The tournament featured eight teams competing in a knockout-style format, with Denmark initially not qualifying. However, just a week before the tournament began, Yugoslavia, which had qualified for the tournament, was forced to withdraw due to international sanctions resulting from the Yugoslav Wars.

As a result of Yugoslavia's withdrawal, UEFA invited Denmark, which had finished second in their qualifying group, to take their place. Despite being a late addition to the tournament and not having played in the qualifying rounds, Denmark accepted the invitation and began their journey in the tournament.

In the group stage, Denmark defeated France and drew with England and Sweden to advance to the knockout stage. In the semi-finals, they beat the reigning champions, the Netherlands, in a penalty shootout. In the final, they faced Germany and won 2-0 with goals from John Jensen and Kim Vilfort, securing their first major international trophy.

Denmark's victory in the Euro 92 tournament is regarded as one of the greatest underdog stories in football history. The team's unexpected success highlighted the importance of teamwork, determination, and belief in the face of adversity. The team's coach, Richard Møller Nielsen, has been credited with creating a winning culture and instilling a sense of unity within the team that helped them achieve their unlikely victory.

6. LA LIGA

185. Which team won the first La Liga title?

186. At what age did Lionel Messi first played for Barcelona?

187. When was the La Liga founded?

188. Which team has the biggest rivalry in La Liga?

189. Which Spanish club won five consecutive La Liga titles between 1991 and 1997?

190. What is the home stadium of Barcelona Football Club?

191. In what year was Barcelona's famous La Masia academy founded?

192. Who is the all-time leading scorer in La Liga for Barcelona Football Club as of 2022?

193. Which La Liga club is based in Seville, Spain?

194. What is the name of the team known as "Los Blancos"?

195. Who is the all-time leading scorer for Real Madrid in La Liga as of 2022?

196. What is the name of the team known as "Los Rojiblancos"?

197. Which La Liga club has the largest stadium in terms of capacity?

198. What is the name of the stadium that is home to Atletico Madrid?

199. Who is the all-time leading scorer in La Liga?

200. What team has won the most La Liga titles?

ANSWERS – LA LIGA

185. FC Barcelona

186. 13

187. 1929

188. Barcelona vs Real Madrid, known as "El Clásico"

189. Barcelona

190. Camp Nou

191. 1979

192. Lionel Messi

7. LIGUE 1

201. In what year was Ligue 1 established?

202. Who won the Ligue 1 Golden Foot award in 2021-2022?

203. Who scored the most number of goals in the history of Ligue 1?

204. Which club did Lionel Messi join in 2021?

205. Who holds the record for the most goals scored in a single Ligue 1 season?

206. Who won the inaugural Ligue 1 Player of the Year?

207. What is the nickname of Marseille?

208. Which club has won the Ligue 1 title the most times in the 2010s?

209. What is the name of the Ligue 1 trophy?

210. Which Ligue 1 club is nicknamed "Les Verts"?

211. How much was the transfer of Neymar from Barcelona to Paris Saint-Germain?

212. Who was the top scorer in Ligue 1 during the 2020/21 season?

213. Which is the first club to win 10 Ligue 1 titles?

214. Which team has won the most consecutive Ligue 1 titles?

215. Which Ligue 1 club has the largest stadium in France?

216. Which country has won the most number of Ligue 1 Player of the Year?

ANSWERS – LIGUE 1

201. 1932

202. Kylian Mbappé

203. Delio Onnis

204. Paris Saint-Germain

205. Josip Skoblar

206. David Ginola

207. Les Phocéens

208. Paris Saint-Germain

209. Trophée des Champions

210. Saint-Étienne

211. £200.5 million

212. Kylian Mbappé

213. Saint-Étienne

214. Paris Saint-Germain

215. Marseille

216. France

8. SERIE A

217. Who is the all-time top scorer in Serie A?

218. Which Serie A club is nicknamed "La Dea"?

219. What year did Serie A start?

220. Which club has the largest stadium in Serie A?

221. Which city is Juventus based in?

222. Who was the Serie A Player of the Year in 2021-2022?

223. AC Milan was hugely successful in the early post-war years due to 3 players known as Gre-No-Li. Which country were the 3 players from?

224. Who was the top scorer in the 2021-2022 Serie A season?

225. Who is the all-time leading scorer for AC Milan in Serie A?

226. Who was the 2021-2022 Serie A Young Player of the Year?

227. Which club has won the most Serie A titles in history?

228. Who won the inaugural Serie A Footballer of the Year?

229. Number 6 in AC Milan is not taken by anyone as an honour to which great player?

230. Who won the 2021-2022 Serie A title?

231. Who won the first Serie A Foreign Footballer of the Year?

232. Who is the first footballer to win the Serie A Footballer of the year award with 2 different teams?

ANSWERS – SERIE A

217. Silvio Piola

218. Atalanta

219. 1898

220. San Siro (AC Milan and Inter Milan)

221. Turin

222. Romelu Lukaku

223. Sweden

224. Cristiano Ronaldo

9. BUNDESLIGA

233. Who was the manager of Borussia Dortmund during the 2010-2011 season when they won the Bundesliga title?

234. What year was Bundesliga founded?

235. Who was the first British player to appear in the Bundesliga?

236. Which club has won the most Bundesliga titles in history?

237. Which animal is on FC Cologne's club crest?

238. What is the name of the stadium that is home to VfB Stuttgart?

239. Who was the first ever Bundesliga champion?

240. Who was the manager of RB Leipzig during the 2016-2017 season when they qualified for the UEFA Champions League for the first time in their history?

241. Who is the all-time leading scorer in Bundesliga history?

242. Which club has the largest stadium in the Bundesliga?

243. What was the first team to beat Bayern Munich in the Bundesliga during the 2020-2021 season?

244. What is RB Leipzig also known as?

245. What is the capacity of the Allianz Arena, the home of Bayern Munich?

246. Which stadium is the home of Schalke 04?

247. Who was the first foreign player to win the Bundesliga top scorer award?

248. Which team has won the most Bundesliga titles in history?

ANSWERS - BUNDESLIGA

233. Jurgen Klopp

234. 1962

235. Kevin Keegan

236. Bayern Munich

237. Goat

238. Mercedes-Benz Arena

239. FC Köln

240. Ralph Hasenhüttl

241. Gerd Muller

242. Signal Iduna Park (Borussia Dortmund)

243. Hoffenheim

244. The Red Bulls

245. 75,000

246. Veltins-Arena

247. Pierre-Emerick Aubameyang

248. Bayern Munich (32 titles)

10. BASILEIRO SERIE A

249. What year was the Campeonato Brasileiro Série A first established?

250. Which is the largest stadium in Brazil?

251. How many teams compete in Campeonato Brasileiro Série A?

252. Which club won the 2021 Basileiro Serie A title?

253. Which club is the first to win 10 Basileiro Serie A titles?

254. Who was the first player to be declared "hors concours" (not being allowed to participate due to being unrivaled by other players) in Basileiro Serie A?

255. Which player has the highest number of appearances in Basileiro Serie A?

256. Which team has the most consecutive Brasileiro Serie A titles?

257. What are matches between Palmeiras and Conrinthians also known as?

258. When was Palmeiras' anthem composed?

259. Who is the first non-Brazilian to win the Brasileiro Serie A manager?

260. What is the nickname of Santos FC?

261. Which club has won the most Brasileiro Serie A titles from 2010 to 2019?

262. Who is the most expensive player in the history of Basileiro Serie A to be transferred to a foreign club?

263. Who is Palmeira's top scorer since its foundation?

264. Which manager is the first to win 3 titles with 3 different teams?

ANSWERS – BASILEIRO SERIE A

249. 1959

250. Maracanã Stadium (Rio de Janeiro)

251. 20

252. Atlético Mineiro

253. Palmeiras

254. Pelé

255. Fábio

256. Santos

11. GOALSCORERS

265. How many goals did Lionel Messi score for Barcelona?

266. Who scored the winning goal in the 2002 World Cup final between Brazil and Germany?

267. Who was the first player to score 100 Premier League goals?

268. Who holds the record for most goals scored in a single World Cup tournament?

269. Who was the first African player to win the Ballon d'Or award?

270. Who is the Premier League's youngest ever goal scorer?

271. Who is the all-time leading scorer for Manchester United in the Premier League?

272. Who was the first player to score 100 goals and 100 assists in Ligue 1?

ANSWERS - GOALSCORERS

265. 672

266. Ronaldo (Brazil)

267. Alan Shearer

268. Just Fontaine (13 goals for France in 1958)

269. George Weah (1995)

270. James Vaughan (16y 270d)

271. Wayne Rooney

272. Dimitri Payet

12. BIZARRE FOOTBALL

273. Who did Zidane headbutt in the 2006 FIFA World Cup?

274. Who did Rangers tried to sign after Alex McLeish was alerted of his ability through popular video game, Football Manager?

275. What is the name of the animal that predicted the 2010 FIFA World Cup results by eating from boxes with flags on?

276. Which Premier League winner's father played rugby for Wales?

277. Which Swedish footballer once had a clause added to his Premier League contract that prohibited him from travelling into space?

278. Which footballer has a galaxy named after him?

279. Who is the most expensive footballer in history, as of 2021?

280. Who is famous for biting other players?

281. Which former international went on to become a professional wrestler in the WWE?

282. What is the informal term for retiring from playing?

283. Which animal is a derogatory term to describe a slow and/or uncreative player?

284. Elton John was twice the owner of which club?

285. Which Spanish club's nickname is Los Colchoneros, translated as "The Mattress Makers" in English?

286. What was the name of the football tournament held in 1950 in Brazil to celebrate the 100th anniversary of Brazil's independence?

287. Which club dominated Italian football before being tragically wiped out in an air crash in May 1949?

288. Which football match was known as the "Battle of Santiago" due to its on-field violence and aggressive play?

ANSWERS – BIZARRE FOOTBALL

273. Marco Materazzi

274. Lionel Messi

275. Paul the Octopus

276. Ryan Giggs

277. Stefan Schwarz

278. Cristiano Ronaldo

279. Kylian Mbappé (€145 million transfer from Monaco to Paris Saint-Germain)

280. Luis Suarez

FUN FACT – THE RITUAL

Bobby Moore, the captain of England's 1966 World Cup-winning team, was known for his meticulous approach to preparation and attention to detail. One of his idiosyncrasies was insisting on being the last player to put his shorts on in the locker room before a match.

Moore believed that this ritual helped him to focus and mentally prepare for the game ahead. He would calmly observe his teammates getting dressed while he waited patiently, and then he would take his time to put on his shorts and socks.

Teammates and opponents alike would marvel at Moore's pre-match routine, and some even found it intimidating. However, Moore was simply doing what he felt was necessary to get himself in the right frame of mind to lead his team to victory.

His method clearly worked, as England went on to win the 1966 World Cup, with Moore lifting the trophy as captain. Moore is still regarded as one of the greatest defenders in football history, and his legacy continues to inspire players and fans to this day.

13. WHO AM I?

289. First English player to win the FIFA World Cup Golden Boot.

290. Voted the "European Player of the Century" in 1999.

291. First goalkeeper to score a Premier League goal.

292. Manager of the "Invincibles" Arsenal team that went the entire 2003-04 season unbeaten in the English Premier League.

293. Youngest head coach in the Bundesliga at 28 years and 205 days.

294. Originally a striker before becoming a defender, and played 11 seasons for the same club before managing them.

295. First footballer to be knighted.

296. Captain of the French national team that won the World Cup in 2018.

297. Oldest FIFA World Cup winning captain at aged forty.

298. First sportsperson to get 10 million followers on Twitter.

299. Only goalkeeper to win the Ballon d'Or award.

300. Won the Champions League with three different clubs.

301. Scored the first "perfect hat-trick" in the Premier League.

302. Won the Premier League with both Leicester City and Manchester City.

303. Won 3 FIFA World Cups.

304. Top scorer 3 times in the 90s when he played for Lazio.

305. Scored the first Premier League hat-trick.

306. First manager to get sacked in Premier League.

307. All-time leading scorer for Chelsea.

308. Only person to score a goal in the 2010 Champions League final between Internazionale and Bayern Munich.

309. First footballer to win the Ballon d'Or, World Cup, and European Cup.

310. First footballer to score 100 international goals.

311. Scored the most goals in a single World Cup tournament.

312. Which former Italian midfielder was nicknamed "The Architect" for his ability to create chances and won the World Cup with Italy in 2006?

ANSWERS – WHO AM I ?

289. Gary Lineker (1986)

290. Johan Cruyff

291. Peter Schmeichel

292. Arsène Wenger

293. Julian Nagelsmann (at Hoffenheim during the 2015/16 season)

294. Jurgen Klopp

295. Sir Stanley Matthews

296. Hugo Lloris

297. Dino Zoff (Italy, 1982)

298. Kaká

299. Lev Yashin

300. Clarence Seedorf

301. Jimmy Floyd Hasselbaink

302. Riyad Mahrez

303. Pelé

304. Giuseppe Signori

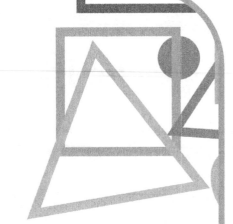

305. Eric Cantona

306. Ian Porterfield

307. Frank Lampard

308. Diego Milito

309. Sir Bobby Charlton

310. Ali Daei from Iran

311. Just Fontaine from France

312. Andrea Pirlo

14. TRUE OR FALSE

313. David Beckham improved his agility during his time at Manchester United by taking ballet lessons.

314. Nicky Byrne, singer in Irish boyban Westlife, played for Leeds United before moving into music.

315. England has won the European Championships at least once as of 2022.

316. Football was the first team sport included in the Olympic Games.

317. Ronaldinho, former Brazil and Barcelona star, spent time in prison after using a fake passport.

318. FIFA World Cup was held during WWII.

319. Cristiano Ronaldo took 27 games to score his first Champions League goal.

320. Pele once starred in a Hollywood movie with Michael Caine and Sylvester Stallone.

ANSWERS – TRUE OR FALSE

313. FALSE

314. TRUE

315. FALSE

316. TRUE

317. TRUE

318. FALSE

319. TRUE

320. TRUE

Printed in Great Britain
by Amazon

20180911R00052